YOUNG

AFTER

40

Unlock Secrets To Reverse Aging Naturally

EDSON BRANDAO

TABLE OF CONTENTS

INTRODUCTION

Billions of dollars are spent annually to preserve health and well-being, even in our downsized economy. The fear of premature aging is a continuing concern of most people in the U.S., especially in the younger and upwardly mobile crowd and even within the generation of baby boomers.

We simply can not avoid the age ravages, yet most people want to age gracefully. One can put off the aging process by leading a healthy life by making smart exercise decisions, eating healthy foods, and reducing your stress levels.

Of course, stress can not be avoided along with the pollution that we breathe every day, and a very unhealthy diet for most people adds to the stress on our bodies and health.

Leading a lifestyle of excess food, drinking, smoking, and late nights out with little or no exercise can radically hasten the appearance of aging, including wrinkles, skin sagging, dark circles, puffiness, and an overall unhealthy look.

We can not prevent the signs of aging if we don't pay attention to our health and personal care. Genetics inevitably plays a major role in our aging. Many people look much younger than their years, although they have not exactly taken care of themselves perfectly. But eventually, their past transgressions begin to catch up with them, and they are forced to take a hard, close look at how they treated their bodies and start a path to repair the damage they have done.

Others may look much older than their ages but still eat healthily and exercise. It may seem almost unfair, but those who look older but maintain their health later will not have to do damage control. You can look youthful and still suffer from various illnesses that may arise from bad health habits. So it is best for those who look younger than their years to take full advantage of the gift they have been given and either take very good care of themselves or immediately get on the health wagon.

Because looking good is a premium in this era, people are spending billions on anti-aging supplements, creams, plastic surgery, Botox, and any number of treatments to keep Father Time from catching up with them. Most people do their best to spend as little as possible, but when a youthful look is desired, money is no object for many. Hormone therapies, antioxidants, specific vitamins, and "natural" herbal supplements promise youth in a bottle. Make sure that you buy the herbal products from companies that you can trust. Random studies have shown some supplements contain very small amounts of the 'magic' elixir they promised to contain within the bottle or capsule.

There are some very good topical products available now in certain stores, including natural health stores in the facial and body product lines. My suggestion would be to try 30 days of a small bottle or jar before you spend hundreds of dollars buying their entire line.

Anti-aging is getting more popular by the day. The supplements work from the inside out and from the outside in, the topical products. People who smoke and love ending up being out in the sun for hours are the ones who seem to age faster than others. They end up with skin and deep lines and wrinkles which look leathery. Back in our country's early days, ladies were all raged about keeping their skin soft, silky, and as pale as possible. Without a very fashionable umbrella, they wouldn't have thought of going out in the sun. Maybe they knew more than we did, and it only took us about 100 years to "get it."

Research has shown time and time again that those who exercise regularly and remain active physically and mentally in their older years show fewer signs of aging than those who live a sedentary lifestyle. Your stamina may increase, your body will be healthier, and your muscle tone and skin will be improved, and you will maintain that much sought-after youthful, vital look.

Plastic surgery, lotions, and potions will help you look younger, But if you don't stay active inside, you'll be forced to pay attention by starting to have problems with your health and mobility. You might look great, but this is all for nothing if you feel bad. Food is a very important part of turning the aging process back or slowing it down.

Fiber-rich foods that help remove cholesterol, eat less 'bad' fats can help with blood pressure and eat little or better yet, no sugar can help with diabetes prevention. That also includes reducing your intake of unhealthy, simple carbohydrates.

A diet rich in dark fruits such as blueberries, acai berries, black raspberries, tart cherries, or any other dark berry contains the so-called anthocyanins. Other anthocyanin-rich foods include many good choices on vegetables such as red cabbage and eggplant. Red wine contains resveratrol that has been found to be very important for good health.

Resveratrol is found in Vaccinium species grapes, wine, grape juice, peanuts, and beers, including blueberries, bilberries, and cranberries. Resveratrol is found only in the skins of grapes. The amount of resveratrol in grape skins varies with the cultivar of grape, its geographic origin, and exposure to infection with fungi.

An important determinant of their resveratrol content is the amount of fermentation time a wine spends in contact with grape skins. White and rosé wines, therefore, generally contain less resveratrol than the red wines. Red or purple grape juices could be good sources of resveratrol as well.

Trans-resveratrol glucoside (trans-priced) is the predominant form of resveratrol in grapes and grape juice, but wines also contain significant amounts of resveratrol aglycones, supposed to be the result of sugar cleavage during fermentation.

Many wines also contain significant amounts of cis-resveratrol, which may be produced or released from vinifera (resveratrol polymers) during fermentation. Red wine is a relatively rich resveratrol source, but other polyphenols are found in red wine at significantly higher concentrations than resveratrol) The total resveratrol content of certain beverages and foods is listed in the table below.

These values should be considered approximate since the content of foods and beverages with resveratrol can vary considerably. (Oregon state.

Exercise can, therefore, keep our skin firm and our bodies tight, well into our old age with good muscle tone. We feel and look good and can extend our lives unless we develop a disease that we don't expect will shorten our life span. If we eat a good and healthy diet by adding more fruits and veggies and less red meat, then after a meal, we'll feel lighter and not feel 'stuffed.' It is known that green and leafy vegetables help us get rid of that excess around the mid-section. Drink little or no of the caffeine, particularly in sodas. They are full of high-fructose corn syrup, and you've been told they're bad for you.

Those over 40 will find that some changes are needed, such as developing new skincare and eating rituals, to stay young. As your skin and body age can help you take a decade or more off your look by changing the way you take your body and style yourself.

Try whitening your teeth. Yellow teeth are a good indication of your age since teeth darken as you age. The effects of coffee, and perhaps smoking, are clearly visible on your teeth by the time you reach 40. A bleaching treatment done at your dentist's office can take almost immediately ten years off of your appearance for serious cases. Otherwise, you will be able to buy special toothpaste and gels for home use.

Control weight. Metabolism is slowing down as you age, especially after 30 years. If you're not up to your exercise intensity, you may end up earning a few pounds a year. That could mean a weight gain of 10 pounds or more by the time you reach 40.

Youth dress up, but don't overdo it. Avoid see-through tops, flashy fabrics, and too-short skirts. You can send the message that you're trying too hard and can actually show your age when wearing this kind of clothing. On the other hand, avoid jeans and baggy clothes from "mom," which will give you the impression you have something to hide. Browse through 40-and-over crowd-oriented fashion magazines that will give you ideas about how to dress up young and keep it classy.

Get your own good bra. Better yet, get a professional bra fitting (available in upscale stores and underwear shops), so you can buy something that's right for you. Because breasts sag when you age (and especially if you've had kids), wearing the right bra takes years off your appearance instantly.

Choose and maintain a hair color that fits your skin tone. Chances are you will have a good amount of gray to cover by the time you reach 40. If you dye a dark tone on your hair, you will need to visit the hair salon more frequently to cover your roots. Lighter colors, or highlighted hair, will hide gray better but might be more expensive to maintain.

Treat skin that is getting older. In your late 30's, deeper lines begin to appear. By 40, you might have to deal with not only more prominent wrinkles but skin discoloration and dryer skin as well. This is the time to discuss prescription creams such as Retin-A, which can get rid of dark spots, lines, and rough skin, with your doctor. Botox or gel fillers may be a better option for the deeper lines. Always wear sunscreen to avoid additional damage.

Switch to makeup, which is lighter. Heavy powder and foundation can sink into wrinkles and lines, making you look older than you are. A softer shadow of the eye and lighter color of the lip will conceal imperfections and minimize attention to problem areas. Before applying a base color, moisturize well, so your skin is well hydrated, and your wrinkles are less likely to show.

There are endless ways to improve and prevent aging. Yes, growing old is just part of our lives, but you can live a long and healthy life with a few 'tweaks' and some good choices and feel great because you can participate in more activities.

AGING GRACEFULLY THROUGH STRESS MANAGEMENT

You know the increasingly old stereotypes. They include decreasing health, energy shortages, a near-zero libido, and countless hours watching television in your last days. The get-older narrative says your knees are supposed to get an ache, your memory and concentration are supposed to decline, and in the morning, you are supposed to crunch and groan out of bed.

Some things slow down as you grow older, and you can't reverse aging, but you can be in peak mental, physical, and emotional health regardless of the stage of life. In your 40s, 50s, 60s, 70s, and beyond, you have significant power to create your very best self.

"The fact is that we've found new ways for scientists to take control of our genes," says Sara Gottfried, MD, in Younger. "For example, diet, exercise, and other lifestyle choices can alter the naughty aging genes typically associated with fat and wrinkles. Simply put, you can actually prevent aging by turning on your good genes and off your bad genes — no matter how old you are.

To age graciously, you don't need to understand genetics, but you have plenty of strategies within your control to do it right. Healthy aging and the cultivation of a vibrant, happy life demands a healthy diet but also effective lifestyle strategies, including stress management.

How Stress Affects Your Health

There are a lot of different types of stress. Chronic stress is when it affects your daily happiness and derails it. Stress can have far-reaching effects, including getting sick more often, social isolation, and speeding up the aging process.

"Stress is probably the single most powerful longevity enemy on the planet," says Jonny Bowden, Ph.D., in The Most Effective Ways of Living Longer, who notes that stress contributes to almost every illness. "Stress can shorten your life, and will."

He names stress among "The Four Horsemen of Aging"—free radicals, Inflammation, and glycation — which can gracefully curtail aging and longevity.

Research confirms that stress can contribute to chronic conditions and diseases, including cardiac disease, cancer, and stroke.

Stress can also often make you sicker. One meta-analysis of over 300 30-year-old empirical articles found a relationship between psychological stress and immunity. Researchers found that acute stressors (such as taking an exam) and chronic stressors (such as constantly worrying about your job status) affected your immune system differently.

More specifically, researchers found that acute stressors, such as situations in combat or flight, could potentially benefit your immune system. Think of those stressors as resilience building. In contrast, chronic stressors can have a detrimental effect on your immune system.

A healthy human body is incredibly adept at handling stressors, yet studies show that your immune system becomes less resilient to these stressors as you age. For example, this can make you less able to respond to vaccines and immune responses, and potentially create early mortality.

"Chronic stress causes your brain to shrink, and your belly to grow," says Mark Hyman, MD, 10-Day Detox Diet in The Blood Sugar Solution. "That's because the main stress hormone, cortisol, damages the brain, shrinking the center of memory (the hippocampus). Our telomeres are shortened by stress, the little end caps on our chromosomes. The shorter the telomeres, the shorter the life.'

While hormonal imbalances underlie stress-related issues — including estrogen, testosterone, and insulin — cortisol is an important player.

"Cortisol is a hormone released during stressful times, be it physical or psychological," says Jason Fung, MD, in The Complete Fasting Guide. "This activates the response to fight or flight — it's an adaptation to survival."

Being stressed chronically keeps cortisol ramped up, which can age you faster.

In Younger, Gottfried describes how, as we grow older, we become less resilient to stress — a poor night's sleep has a more detrimental effect as you age. She calls the inflammatory process: "the unfortunate hybrid of increasing inflammation, stiffness and aging."

"Too much cortisol and you become insulin resistant and store fat in your belly," Hyman says.

GROWTH HORMONE: THE KEY HORMONE TO AGING GRACEFULLY

Somatotropin, more commonly known as growth hormone, is another key hormonal player involved in stress-aging, which Bowden calls "the ultimate anti-aging hormone."

Low growth hormone levels are becoming a sure way of aging you. Research shows side effects include decreased muscle mass and ability to exercise, increased visceral fat, impaired quality of life, increased risk of cardiovascular disease, decreased bone mass, and increased mortality. In other words, deficient growth hormone levels become a virtually guaranteed way of not aging gracefully.

One study found older carers with chronic stress had lower levels of growth hormone. Researchers believe these levels explained in part why they responded poorly to the influenza vaccine and suffered delayed healing of the wound.

"Replacing growth hormone in older people with low levels has significant anti-aging benefits," says Fung, who adds unwanted side effects of growth hormone replacement therapy. You want to boost growth hormone naturally, instead, more ways to do it in one minute.

Balance becomes the key to cortisol, growth hormone, and other hormones being managed and optimized. It becomes a crucial way to learn to roll with stress.

Simply put, your hormones become imbalanced when you're stressed out, which accelerates aging. The good news is you've got lots of tools to manage stress and age gracefully.

12 STRESS MANAGEMENT TIPS TO AGE GRACEFULLY

A key component of gracefully growing old is learning to manage stresses. How to manage and relieve stress plays an important role in healthy aging.

"The key point is that the right food, sleep, exercise, and detoxification can reverse many age-related hormone problems," Gottfried says in Younger. Here are 12 ways to gracefully manage stress and age.

1. EAT MORE FRUITS AND VEGETABLES

One Australian study with more than 60,000 adults over 45 found that increasing fruits and vegetables could help middle-aged and older adults reduce psychological distress. A wide range of antioxidant-rich, colorful products, including leafy green vegetables and berries, can reduce the oxidative stress that Bowden says accelerates aging, among their benefits.

2. DRINK MORE GREEN TEA

Green tea could be the ideal way to reduce stress and age well. Researchers are showing that polyphenols in green tea can protect your skin from premature aging, and L-theanine can lower levels of stress. Look for organic green tea, and then opt for decaffeinated varieties if you are sensitive to caffeine.

3. GET THE RIGHT NUTRIENTS

Researchers find foods rich in age-related diseases such as atherosclerosis, cardiovascular disease, cancer, and dementia can be protected by polyphenols. Resveratrol has positive effects as anti-aging compounds through the modulation of oxidative damage, Inflammation, attrition of the telomere, and other markers of aging. You will probably want to supplement therapeutic amounts of resveratrol and other potentially anti-aging nutrients. Talk with your chiropractor or another health professional to include the right doses of resveratrol and other anti-aging nutrients in your diet

4. NIX THE SUGAR

For stress management and healthy aging, sugar should be avoided. Sticks and crashes of blood sugar, causing mood swings and low energy — but that is only part of the problem. Glycation, which Bowden says helps you grow old, occurs when your proteins get too much sugar "gum up," making them adhesive and ineffective in their work. Glycation creates advanced glycation end products, properly known as AGEs, which contributes to numerous conditions, including skin aging. Sugar is available in sneaky form — including almond milk in healthy foods — so read labels and ingredients. Put it back if it has more than five grams of sugar per serving.

5. LOWER INFLAMMATION

Research shows that many Americans eat 20 times or more of the omega-6 fatty acids than omega-3 fatty acids anti-inflammatory. The results are shown around our waistline and health overall. Inflammation is linked to a number of diseases, including obesity. Inflammatory foods include possible food sensitivities – like milk or gluten – as well as high-grade foods such as vegetable oil in omega-6 fatty acids. Focus instead on anti-inflammatory, nutrient-rich foods, including wild-caught seafood, fresh ground linens, chia seeds, berries, leafy non-starchy, and cruciferous plants.

6. TRY MEDITATION

One of the advantages of meditation in reducing stress, a study of 40 teachers from secondary schools who tutored children with behavioral problems, found transcendental meditation helped teachers and support staff to reduce psychological distress.

7. STAY FLEXIBLE WITH YOGA

Evidence has shown that yoga can improve muscle strength and endurance, encourage or enhance breathing and cardiovascular function, minimize stress, anxiety, depression, and chronic pain, improve sleep habits, and improve overall well-being and quality of life. Besides meditation, there are many various types of yoga, including gentle yoga, vinyasa flow, and hot yoga. Finding the style that works for you might involve sampling some classes or experiment online. Breathing is also a key component of yoga that reduces stress and allows you to age gracefully.

8. LIFT WEIGHTS

"As we get older, we lose our muscle — it just gets wasted," Hyman says in Food: How do I feed the Heck? 'This occurs as a result of our bodies developing lower testosterone and growth hormones and elevated stress hormone levels of cortisol.' Weight resistance is an effective way of counteracting muscle loss, minimizing tension and moving (and staying) into and out of mid-life. You don't need a lot of time to gain. Stellar outcomes can also be obtained in 15–20 minutes a few days a week. The form is crucial, so please work with a personal trainer, especially if you are new to lifting weight. Injuring yourself causes more pain only!

9. GET MORE SLEEP

The growth hormone is released mainly during the deepest levels of sleep. When you don't get deep and relaxing sleep regularly, you could not make enough of this hormone. Sleep deprivation can also keep the following evening's cortisol levels elevated and impact the strength of your stress response. Sleeping enough — about 8 hours deep, uninterrupted sleep — needs good hygiene of sleep. It involves shutting off devices one or two hours before bed and avoiding something disrupting sleep.

10. TRY INTERMITTENT FASTING

You will increase growth hormone efficiently without a potentially harmful hormone replacement. "The most effective natural stimulus to secrete the growth hormone is fasting," Fung says. "In one study, growth hormone secretion more than doubled in a five-day fasting cycle." If you are new to fasting, try intermittent fasting a few times a week. Dinner shut the kitchen for the night, and force breakfast as late in the morning as possible. You will have a 14-hour or longer fasting period, which will naturally increase the growth hormone and help you lose weight.

11. EAT MORE QUALITY PROTEIN

"Protein is needed for muscle maintenance and building, and age-related hormonal changes, elevated blood pressure hormonal levels such as cortisol and lower anti-aging levels of hormones such as growth hormone and testosterone occur with the loss of muscle," says Hyman in Food. "These are the reasons why studies show that more protein is required for disease and death prevention when you are aged." Smart protein sources include poultry of free reach, grass-fed beef, and wild-caught seafood. Vegans and vegetarians can derive large quantities of high-quality protein from foods such as legumes, nuts, and seeds.

12. VISIT YOUR CHIROPRACTOR

You should consult your chiropractor, one of the greatest ways to decrease tension and mitigate or reverse several aging elements — including

Inflammation, oxidative stress, pain relief, and a powerful immune system. Chiropractic treatment provides optimal longevity and stress management. In addition to treating spinal malalignments, the chiropractor will build a customized routine to keep you safe, lean, and vibrating as you get older.

Chronic stress can, in so many ways, ruin your life, like aging. Self-care is not a luxury, nor learning how to cope with stress if you intend to mature graciously. With these 12 main tactics, you have what you need to make your self feel older.

EXERCISES AND REGULAR WORKOUT TO LOOK YOUNGER

The strength of an ongoing exercise regimen is impressive: daily activity will help you develop stronger muscles, control chronic illnesses, and boost the health of your garment. Yet there's another advantage of the physical exercise that deserves a shouting: how many birthdays you've celebrated only in small amounts appear to take years off your age. You can't alter your biological age, of course, but exercise might make you look and feel younger than you are, says Frank Frisch, Ph.D., Chair of Kinetics at Chapman University in Orange, California.

Taking into account the 15 physical and emotional effects of a sweat session on the brain and body. Using this list would never again inspire you to take a workout.

BENEFITS OF REGULAR WORKOUTS TO LOOK YOUNGER

The benefits of physical exercise are impressive: they help to strengthen the joints, develop muscles, enhance immunity, and reduce disease. Nevertheless, there is another compelling explanation of why you should work out every day – they help you look and feel younger. No matter how many birthdays you celebrate, when you're finished on a regular basis, practice will make you look younger and fitter for your age.

Besides incredible physicality and strength, you should know some other benefits of exercise. Understanding the main problems in the list below will empower you to adhere to a daily workout schedule and take full advantage of exercise.

EXERCISE GIVES YOU MORE STRENGTH AND ENERGY

Exercises are like a strong, chemically flavored energy drink. During each session, you fire your brain and body and feel more relaxed and active. Only a quick 30-minute cardiovascular workout will make you feel mentally and physically healthier and fresher.

To beginners, exercise can be painful and strenuous, but if you exercise every day, your workouts will be quick. The more relaxed and dedicated you are in your routine, the more you start enjoying it-so, the more you can take your body off. Not miss the workouts only because there is no time to visit the fitness center or outdoors. You can also set up your own mini fitness center in your garage using the most appropriate investment equipment.

EXERCISE KEEPS YOUR SKIN YOUTHFUL AND GLOWING

The sweat that drips your brow may not be the only thing that brings your skin shine. Exercise is, in many ways, beneficial to the skin. The sweat cleans the skin of toxins and opens the pores to allow airflow. This also increases the elasticity of the skin, which can be easily observed in a person aged 40 + years.

EXERCISE GIVES YOU MORE VIM AND VIGOR

A workout is like the energy drink of nature, tossing up your mind and body so that you feel more alert and alive. "Exercise positions the body in an enjoyable state that translates into more energy and a sense of well-being," says Frisch. "Day activities are less challenging and take less energy." It's the kind of spice in your move that makes you feel like a decade or two has peeled off.

EXERCISE KEEPS YOUR SKIN SOFT AND GLOWING

Due to the moisture that drips off your forehead, a dewy glow is not the only way to keep your skin fresh. McMaster University researchers in Ontario surveyed a diverse sample of adults aged 20 to 84 years of age. The regular exercisers over the age of 40 had skin that looked like people's soft, elastic skin in the 20s and

30s. The distinction was not with sun exposure (who would age the skin quickly if you did not wear sunscreen), the research team reported. They theorized that exercise releases physical substances that help delay the aging of the skin.

EXERCISE IMPROVES YOUR POSTURE

Due to the loss of muscle and improvements in bone density, your posture will affect you as you age. Compete with strength training that improves muscle and bone health, particularly in your heart and spinal cord, so that you naturally stand and shave your appearance longer and longer, says Amie Hoff, personal coach and founder of Hoff Fitness in New York City. You also feel physically more positive when working out, and you automatically stop feeling tired and straightening up, "she says.

EXERCISE IMPROVES YOUR FLEXIBILITY

Aging doesn't only make your views more inflexible — it also strengthens your muscles and joints so that you feel stiff and rickety. Regular practice sessions, especially stretch-oriented workouts such as yoga and pilates, keep you loose and bendy, says Hoff. "If aerobic workouts are your preference, you can increase your flexibility by warming up and refreshing with foam roller exercises," she suggests. This foam exercise tool removes muscle nodes and reduces stiffness.

EXERCISE BOOSTS YOUR MOOD

You've heard about the rider's highness, and a positive mood boost will happen during any aerobic sweat training. This appears to come down to endorphins: when you're involved, the chemicals in your body churn out. Eric Sternlicht, Ph.D., associate professor of kinesiology at Chapman University, says, "Endorphins are like real opiates." Some evidence suggests that gymnastics can cause changes to other neurotransmitters correlated with positive emotions, including dopamine. And the confidence you get allows you to be more secure too.

EXERCISE HELPS YOU SLEEP SOUNDLY

Restless sleep is like a young waterfall, and practice allows you to make it happen. "Evidence indicates that daily exercisers sleep well and undergo deep REM sleep," says Frisch. You definitely need a heart-pounding workout, but there's more to it than that. Well-sleeping allows all the processes to function optimally so that you feel less anxious and then toss and turn all night long.

New research has shown that having at least 150 minutes of exercise a week increases the quality of sleep by 65%.

EXERCISE KEEPS YOUR METABOLISM HIGH

Metabolism gradually slows as you age, and it's difficult to resist rising pounds over the years. Luckily scheduling daily workouts helps you increase the overall amount of calories you consume to maintain a steady, healthy weight. You're going to burn more calories if you add a lot of strength training to your routine at least a few days a week because working out with free weights or bodyweight exercises helps develop muscle mass. "And it stays higher during the day, right when you stop training."

EXERCISE SLOWS CELL AGING

Exercise does not only make you feel younger; it will also stop the mechanism of aging in your chromosomes. This is linked to the telomeres that regulate aging at the end of chromosomes. Telomeres become shorter as you grow older, and longevity is associated with longer telomeres. Recent studies have established a link between physical exercise and lengthening the telomeres, meaning that exercise will slow down and help you live longer. "While exercise does not guarantee a long life, it can increase your chances greatly," says Frisch.

EXERCISE REDUCES BELLY FAT

As you go into the middle age, fat mostly on your hips and thighs starts appearing more and more along the abdomen, particularly after menopause. This is real. This visceral fat, as it is called, may increase your risk of chronic conditions such as diabetes and heart disease, in comparison to fat on other body areas. It's persistent, but it appears to be minimized or removed by daily workout sessions. A 2011 study from Duke University found that aerobic exercise would cause more belly fat loss than strength training or a combination of strength and cardiovascular training.

EXERCISE RELIEVES STRESS

A long outdoor run or picturesque walk will distract you from fear and anxiety. Yet exercising physiologically can reduce stress. "The release of endorphins through exercise has a calming effect and decreases anxiety," Zonoozi says. Further meditative activities, such as yoga or Tai Chi, promote consciousness and move the body. Staying in the moment while you concentrate on breathing and pulse pace makes it much easier to get emotionally anxious about a difficult job or to argue with a friend last night.

EXERCISE ENHANCES YOUR MEMORY

Through the years, it's natural to get forgotten. Nevertheless, work shows that you can battle exercise against brain fog. Researchers who wrote in the British Sports Medicine Journal in 2014 also concluded that routine aerobic exercise appears to have improved memory-related hippocampus capacity. Earlier research has also associated preparation with sharper cognitive abilities. When you have older moments these days, turn them back on the treadmill.

EXERCISE MAKES YOUR HEART MORE EFFICIENT

Like all muscles, the heart is sluggish and inactive. As a result, you have to work harder to pump your blood throughout the body, add more stress, and feel fatigued and winded. Good even a moderately vigorous workout (like a fast 30-minute walk) will boost your heart to pump oxygen-rich blood into your body more effectively, resulting in less stress, says Rhonda

Zonoozi, a physiologist at Sun Health and Wellness Center in Arizona, and a licensed health and wellness coach.

EXERCISE PROTECTS YOU FROM HEART DISEASE

The heart-healthy effects of exercise don't end there. Daily exercise often raising the risk for age-related cardio complications, such as high blood pressure and high triglyceride levels, a form of blood fat that can block or harden the arteries. They are the main contributors to heart disease, according to the CDC, the number one murderer among men and women. "Exercise also increases HDL levels or good cholesterol, the sort that protects the heart against cardiovascular disease," says Zonoozi.

EXERCISE IMPROVES YOUR BLOOD FLOW

When you age, not only can joints get steeper – the body's blood vessels can lose their flexibility. This makes it more difficult for them to expand to provide oxygen-rich blood (such as the brain, heart, and muscles) as needed, and stronger arteries will raise blood pressure so that the heart has to work harder to pump blood through them. Exercise can reduce blood pressure and increase circulation, and some research indicates even basic relaxation — thinking yoga, pilates, or any relaxing movements — can help enhance blood vessel strength.

BEST EXERCISES FOR MEN IN 40S

1. STANDARD PLANKS

These workouts are one of the most accurate and easy to do in your 40s. It increases strength, and you can boost your balance and stamina. Yet note to do it

correctly

2. BARBELL SQUATS

Those are a compound lifting exercise that focuses primarily on the entire trunk, but also support the upper body and heart. You should try not to use heavy loads, which may cause damage – focus on stability with moderate weight and ensure that the knees and lower back are formed properly to avoid injuries.

3. LYING DOWN LEG LIFTS

This workout is directed at the core muscles and the body's hip flexors that lose strength as you age. The hanging leg raise is a variation of this movement that can lead to tension over the shoulders if it is done too much. It reduces stress on your body and helps you focus more on the things you need to work on.

4. ELLIPTICAL TRAINING

An elliptical system is a fitness machine, but it also helps to increase strength. Running sounds like a good option, but it may be too hard for your knees and legs – ellipticals can allow you to concentrate more on your arms and core strength. You can do this exercise to good effect a single workout for as much as an hour.

5. PUSH-UPS

Push-ups are a classic chest movement that can be done almost without training. We focus on strength in the upper body and strengthen the body's balance. You will even put the biceps and triceps into a number of muscles, including the heart to leg muscles. A full exercise, make sure you do as much as possible as it is a resistance exercise.

6. YOGA

Yoga may not be the "coolest" choice for those who used to be gym rats when they were younger – but you are old enough to no longer care about what is "cool." Yoga is the ideal low-impact exercise routine since it works on physical endurance as much as on flexibility and mental health.

7. HIKING

It could be the perfect way to have fun when you're doing a workout simultaneously. You will enjoy the beautiful outdoors around you and make it more enjoyable for yourself by slowly increasing the distance each time you go on hiking. Walking is a great aerobic exercise that helps you to work out all of your big body muscle groups. It is more an opportunity than a leisurely Sunday practice to get the job finished.

8. RUNNING ROUTINES

The King of Cardio exercises, even though you are in your 40s, still work. It is one of the easiest ways to maintain weight while preserving your heart's health. You should try to ease it because your body is not what it used to be – try always to properly fit yourself with good shoes and a high surface to run on.

EXERCISES THAT MEN SHOULD AVOID AFTER THE 40s

Some activities can also be kept from when you are older than 35 or 40. Any of them are listed below.

1. Sit-ups

It's one of the toughest workouts an older adult can do, despite the stress they put on their legs. You can injure your bottom back or even herniate from all the heat. For greater impact, you can substitute these with planks and side planks.

2. Dead-lifts

Although they appear to be quite macho, they are one of the worst things that you can do to your body in your 40s – in particular, if you do not have prior experience. The body will end up succumbing to a lot of injuries without knowing the form and having the heart.

3. Rows with Rotation

This is a great exercise when you are younger to strengthen your back muscles, but you could push a disk again if you do it wrong.

4. Russian Twists

Your lumbar spine will give your body stability and not mobility – if you drag it under stress for long enough, after some time, it will become dangerous for your body.

5. Overhead Presses

Often, this has to do with the way the individual performs this rather than the exercise. When not done properly, you could end up severely damaging your lower back.

6. Leg Press

Leg presses are a great exercise for men's buttocks, if the range of motion is too much, it will put a lot of stress on your lower back, and this can cause nagging back pain that is incredibly difficult to handle.

10 EXERCISES WOMEN OVER 40 CAN DO TO FEEL 20 YEARS YOUNGER

The body starts to weaken around 30, but exercise can not only delay aging, but it can also undo some of the harm that has already been done over time. We have thus established an exercise regimen that addresses the most common diseases and progressive health problems that begin to occur after 40. After all, everyone needs to know the secret to feel like they're again in their 20s.

1. GRAB YOUR FEET WITH YOUR HANDS WHILE ARCHING YOUR BACK TO DIMINISH MUSCLE PAIN.

This posture helps pump blood and oxygenate the body, reducing muscle pain.

What to do:

- Lie on a comfortable surface of your stomach. When you have one on hand, you can use a yoga mat.
- Bend your knees toward your head.
- Turn your arms back and grab your legs while keeping your head up and your eyes looking forward.
- Stay in this position for 10 seconds.
- Rest for 10 seconds, and repeat ten times.

2. JUMP ROPE TO KEEP YOUR HEART STRONG.

Jumping rope is easy, but it can do wonders to keep your heart healthy away from cardiovascular issues.

What to do:

- Grab each end of a rope with your hands.
- Raise your arms and leap over the arched rope under your feet, easily.

- Instead, the arms should go back to their initial location. Answer fifteen times.
- Rest for 10 seconds. Do five sets of 15 jumps.

3. PUNCH + KICK TO KEEP OSTEOPOROSIS AWAY.

It is a high-intensity exercise that, contrary to what you would expect, helps create bone structure, and prevents osteoporosis-induced damage.

What to do:

- While standing up, lift your right knee.
- Elevate the right foot and leg rapidly in a kicking motion. You should have your leg straight at the start of the jump.
- Return to the standing position.
- Take a big step forward with your knee bent right, when kicking your left arm.
- Return to the standing position. Do three sets of 15.

4. TRY THIS "SUPERMAN" POSE TO REDUCE THE RISK OF DEVELOPING ARTHRITIS.

Such strength training provides the risk of developing arthritis and experiencing joint pain.

What to do:

- Lay on your stomach with your arms extended forward, on a comfortable surface.
- Hold the legs straight and together and lift them between 4 and 8 in from the floor.

- At the same time, heave your arms together. They will also be in size from the floor at around 4 to 8.
- Maintain this position for 10 seconds.
- • Return to starting place. Rest 10 seconds. You need to repeat ten times.

5. LIFT WEIGHTS WHILE LAYING DOWN TO KEEP BACK PAIN AWAY.

Strengthening your core muscles helps to hold your back under any weight and tension, reducing back pain.

What to do:

- Lie on your back with your legs bent over a comfortable surface.

- You should have your arms wide open and carry a heavy object like kettlebells or small weights.
- Raise your arms over your shoulders, and touch them.
- Bring your hands back on the floor. If you want more flexibility in the exercise, return your arms to the initial position without hitting the floor.
- Repeat ten times throughout the cycle. Rest a minute. Do 5 10 sets.

6. COMMIT TO A SET OF LEG DEADLIFTS TO PREVENT MUSCLE LOSS.

It has been demonstrated that strength exercise, such as leg deadlifts, prevents and even recovers muscle loss.

What to do:

- Stand up, bend your back at an angle of 90 °, and let your arms hang.

- Raise your right leg until your body forms a straight line to the table, supporting yourself on your left side. You can feel muscles contracting in your legs. Return your leg to the starting position.

51

- Repeat 20 times. Rest for one minute.
- Do the same movement with the opposite leg. Do two sets.

7. DO SITTING SQUATS TO HOLD YOUR BODY, WHILE PROTECTING YOUR KNEES.

Some women can feel that squats put too much pressure on their knees, but as it is the perfect exercise to sculpt your lower body, with this modification, you can still try it.

What to do:

- Stand up with a chair behind you.
- Separate your feet to hip-width apart.
- Bend your legs as though you were about to sit down and lean on your chair for a second. Keep your heart close, and hold your back straight.
- Return to the initial position. Do three sets of 20 squats.

8. START A BRISK WALKING SCHEDULE TO KEEP YOUR BODY OXYGENATED AND YOUR SKIN CELLS LOOKING NEW.

Speed walking is one of the best workouts you can do when you're over 40 as it greatly decreases the risk of developing heart attacks, increases the ability of your body to consume oxygen and reduces the risk of breaking your bone. It is also considered a form of beauty therapy as it encourages oxygen to enter your skin cells and slows down the cycle of aging. Plus, it's safe, it doesn't need training, and you can do it anywhere you want.

What to do:

- Hurry up, walking. Don't jog or sprint, just walk fast.
- Take a minute's break if you need it, and then carry on.
- Do this for 30 minutes.

9. USING ELASTIC BANDS TO GET YOUR METABOLISM BACK UP FAST.

People performing resistance workouts have a more efficient metabolism, which helps them to consume more calories on average every day.

What to do:

- Take both ends of your resistance band and put the band under your right foot.
- Keep your back straight, raise your arms, hold your hands up to your back.
- Put down your hands and repeat the motion ten times.
- Shift the legs ten times, then repeat the movement.
- Tie the feet together and bring the band underneath. Repeat the movement ten times.

10. *AVOID A ROUNDED BACK WITH THE HELP WITH A FRIEND.*

Correct the stance with this yoga pose, and avoid a rounded back. Your yoga partner will help you stabilize your spine and neck slowly and with a light pressure, which will hold the hump away.

What to do:

- Lie straight on your back underneath and cross your legs.
- Let your friend sit with his legs straight behind you and his feet on the lower back.
- Put your arms behind you, and take the hands of your friend. You should be feeling a little pressure on your back.
- Your friend should put his feet on your back a little higher and keep them going up until they hit the peak of your spine. And then again, they would go all the way down.
- Repeat five times.

YOUR ULTIMATE 7-DAY PLAN

This schedule incorporates everything into one timetable that is easy to follow:

DAY 1

- 30-minute cardio
- 30-minute yoga

DAY 2

- 45-minute intervals/cardio

DAY 3

- 20 minute of weight training
- 30-minute yoga

DAY 4

- 30-minute cardio
- 30-minute yoga

DAY 5

- 45-minute intervals/cardio
- 20-minute weight training

DAY 6

- 30 min cardio
- 30 min yoga

DAY 7

- Take a REST

FAQ'S

Some questions you might have included:

1. HOW OFTEN SHOULD 40+ MEN WORKOUT?

You will work out 4-5 days a week with 2-3 days of strength training, including 3-4 days of aerobic training.

2. CAN I GAIN MUSCLE ONCE I CROSS 40?

You can add muscle, of course-but you know the process is much harder. Your body slows down with age, and muscle mass, along with bone density, appears to start rising after age 30 to 40. Maintaining the current muscle mass would be a challenge, and if you want muscle benefit, you will have to work harder.

3. IS CARDIO BAD FOR MEN OVER 40?

Cardio is not harmful to men-however; with any exercise, it can turn out that it has a detrimental effect on overall health.

4. WHICH EXERCISE IS BEST TO DO AT HOME FOR MEN?

Planks, push-ups, and lungs all function a lot of different muscle groups, and when it comes to improving your overall fitness, they're hard to beat.

There's no question that when you're in your 30s and 40s, you can continue to exercise – but please try to make sure that the form is correct because the body becomes more delicate than ever.

HERE ARE 10 FACE EXERCISES YOU LOOK YOUNGER HELPS:

1. TURKEY NECK TIGHTENER

This list is about the face, but it's also important to have a toned neck to make you look younger. This anti-sagging exercise battles the scary wrinkle-looking "turkey neck" that we can get if we don't do some anti-aging exercises on the face and back.

Raise your chin, tip your head back until the skin is taut under your jaw. Move your lower jaw, press your tongue to the lower line of your gum and stretch out your lower lip.

2. UNDER EYE LIFTER

These bags under your eyes do not show enough rest, but this easy exercise in the face will make you look younger, quicker. Look up with your eyes only until you feel a pressure, without moving or tilting your head. This will sound like you are looking at both eyebrows' heart. As you look up, the eyelids can flutter while putting a strain on an understated muscle. When doing this exercise for naturally looking younger, try to breathe deeply.

3. CHEEK APPLE LIFTER

A research study showed that after corrective dental surgery, smile muscle training could enhance muscle tone and create respect about how patients feel about their social appearance. But think of it as a happy exercise.

If you have one, pinch the corner of your mouth with clean hands, near where your smile line should be. Smile as wide as you can, while pinching tightly enough to encounter pressure (but not hurting yourself). You'll feel a tug that raises the apples of your cheeks in your facial muscle. Try having one side at a time.

4. UPPER EYE LIFTER

The eyes are the windows to the soul, and the main anti-aging effect positive thinking readers want to see is a boost in the eye area. Place your fingertips close to the lower brow line of both eyebrows using the three middle fingers on both hands. Push in and gently push up with your fingers while the eyebrows frown and create resistance.

5. JOWL LIFTER

Lift your neck out like in the exercise of the turkey neck. Turn your head to either side and stick your lower jaw out.

6. NECK LINE DEFINER

Shift your neck to either side until the longitudinal muscles and tendons of your neck are visible in the mirror. Such vertical lines enable a slender neck to elongate and form, making you look younger. Keep this pose on either hand for ten seconds.

7. COLLAR BONE DEFINER

The collar bone is an area that accentuates a young face and neck base, and it's a hard place to tone. With your neck turned like in the neckline definer exercise, twist your opposite shoulder forward about two or three inches until you see a hollow form in a triangular formation between the neck and arm. Repeat on both hands.

8. FOREHEAD LINE ERASER

Push the fingertips on both hands softly up at your hairline while slightly frowning. Do not wrinkle your nose, but frown, so you force it down enough to create resistance to pushing your fingers upward.

9. NOSTRIL TO UPPER LIP LINE ERASER

Place your thumbs clean inside your upper cheek close to your gums. Smile, you close your upper lip to press your thumbs down.

10. CHIN LIFTER

Only roll your lower lip over your teeth to smooth your nose. Place your tongue between your teeth and your lower lip and press your lower lip on your tongue.

FOODS THAT MAKE YOU LOOK YOUNGER AT 40

8 WAYS CHANGING YOUR DIET CAN MAKE YOU LOOK 10 YEARS YOUNGER

Although there is currently no way to defy nature and switch back time, it is perfectly possible to roll back the clock on your looks. If you believe the cliche, "you're what you're eating," then it must also be valid that your diet shows on your face.

In reality, nixing up some grub and moving your diet towards healthier, whole foods will work wonders on your youthfulness — from erasing nasty fine lines to instantly giving you a healthy glow.

1. You'll Prevent Sun Damage

If you're one to stay too long worshipping the summer sun, you may want to add lycopene-rich foods to your diet — think tomatoes, papaya, and grapefruit. A study published in the British Journal of Dermatology showed that the potent antioxidant showed in tomato paste protected the skin from extreme photodamage, which can turn into irregular skin texture and age spots.

2. You'll Improve Skin Elasticity

Tossing a handful of crushed walnuts over your morning oats or mid-afternoon salad does more than just quell tummy grumbling, it can also help speed up the development of collagen — the most abundant protein in our bodies that helps keep skin plump, healthy and youthful — thanks to the high omega-3 content.

3. You'll Bypass Premature Aging

Approximately 75 percent of the fat in olive oil is monounsaturated fatty acids that can play a role in improving youth. "Antioxidant polyphenols in olive oil may also quench dangerous free radicals." Omega-3 fatty acids are also important to keep your skin dewy and hydrated from the inside, so be sure to keep wild-caught salmon, herring, and sardines on your weekly turn.

4. Your Zits Will Zap Away

Loading up with foods such as kale and carrots on vitamin A (the same ingredient used in topical Retin-A treatment) is a perfect way to encourage skin cell turnover, which is essential to avoiding wrinkles and battling acne.

5. You'll Decrease Inflammation

Sneaky signs can also show up on your skin when you are suffering from chronic inflammation.

Inflammation-related symptoms such as redness, eczema, and flare-ups of psoriasis can be greatly alleviated by simply removing insulin-spiking refined carbs such as white bread, white rice, and cereals. Another helpful hint: "There is no topical product that can reduce inflammation in the dermis, but diet has been shown to reduce inflammation, particularly if these goals can be achieved, supplemented with fish oil and polyphenols."

6. You'll Smoothen Out Wrinkles

It's no secret that crow's feet and lines of laughter add years to your profile. There is, however, a surefire way of combating unsightly wrinkles that do not entail an expensive visit to a plastic surgeon. "Focus on a healthy diet with plenty of lean vegetables and protein and avoid sugar, " Bad diets high in sugar have been related to advanced end products for glycation (AGEs), which cause wrinkles and loss of collagen and elastin.

7. It'll Keep Your Skin Flake-Free

Cold winter months in the form of uncomfortable flakes and scales will take a very unappealing toll on your skin. Loading up with vitamin C is a simple way to counteract the flakes. Work published in the American Journal of Clinical Nutrition indicates that people who have foods high in vitamin C in their diet have fewer wrinkles and less dry skin linked to age than those who don't. Not to mention, vitamin C helps to develop collagen that is fond of the skin. Next time you need a pick-me-up afternoon, peel an orange back or brighten up your usual salad by tossing in strawberries, red peppers, and grapefruit.

8. You'll Glow From Within

We are all aware that harmful ultraviolet rays can cause havoc on our bodies. But, there's a sunny lining: By eating beta-carotene-rich foods like carrots, spinach, and sweet potatoes, you can get the glow without damage. "They give you a nice, moist glow and it helps to combat the salty skin of being sick, cold and flu, or doldrums in winter,"

FOODS THAT MAKE YOU LOOK YOUNGER

1. Shiitake mushrooms

The look of salt-and-pepper undoubtedly adds gravitas, but it also belies age. And, if you're not at — or would like to look younger than — the right age (for most people, graying will start about mid-40s), it's an easy fix. Copper deficiency is one of the main causes of premature graying, according to a study in Biological Trace Mineral Science. Slate more shiitake mushrooms into your diet to raise your levels; only one cup of the fungi contains more than 100 percent of the recommended daily value.

2. Sardines

When you age, one nutrient reigns when it comes to holding your muscles taut: protein. However, some main protein sources — red meat in particular — have aging effects, due to high levels of fat and LDL cholesterol (that is the bad type). Instead, get your protein, including sardines, from a low-fat, balanced source. They are also supplied with Omega-3s as a bonus, helping to minimize LDL cholesterol and Vitamin B12, helping to improve cardiovascular function. The only difficult part is to find out how to make those gross fish stomach.

3. Greek yogurt

If you would prefer to receive your protein from a non-aquatic source, you could do much worse than a Greek yogurt aid. This is filled with protein, for one thing. But the stuff in vitamin B12 is high too. In fact, according to the Harvard Medical School study, there are only two 6-ounce portions of simple, nonfat Greek yogurt, which contain the daily recommended amount of vitamin B12.

4. Maca root

If you haven't heard of the foodie phenomenon du jour, you're forgiven. But maca root has become increasingly popular in recent years, thanks to its quasi-magical skin-boosting properties. The material is filled with riboflavin, niacin, and vitamin B6, both of which have been shown to facilitate skin cell regeneration, according to High Altitude Medicine and Biology. You can get your maca fix from smoothies (through the form of powder), pastries (either your own health-conscious bakeshop or your own recipes), or add-ons.

5. Rosemary

Phytonutrients are present in everything that goes through photosynthesis — also called phytochemicals —. Phytonutrients are believed to improve the ceramide content of your skin, which, according to the American Journal of Clinical Dermatology, leads to healthier, cleaner, youthful skin. And you can not top rosemary when it comes to having the best bang for your dollar. The flavoring herb produces over a dozen phytonutrients.

6. Plum tomatoes

Any skincare professional would tell you that sunscreen is your greatest friend when it comes to maintaining your skin's health. But by eating loading up on tomatoes, you can reap the benefits of sunscreen. According to research in the British Journal of Dermatology, people who get about five tablespoons of tomatoes a day will see a reduction of up to 33 percent in UV absorption. What's more, tomatoes, in particular plum tomatoes, are filled with antioxidants that speed up the production of collagen. (Collagen gives plump, soft skin.)

7. Turmeric

Fact: All needs to remove coffee stains for decades. (Indeed, according to a recent survey, almost 90 percent of Americans will give up a pleasure — whether it's candy or holiday — for a whole year to have whiter teeth.) But the most effortless alternative to whiter, younger chompers don't need a pack of pricey white stripes. Simply brush your teeth with turmeric instead. Owing to the intrinsic abrasive properties of the orange paste, brushing your teeth with the material will only scrape back enough enamel to avoid stains.

8. Dark chocolate

Lovers of chocolate (so, everyone), happy: your favorite treat is legally good. In addition to the well-known benefits of BP cutting, chocolate can also help firm up the skin, according to studies in the Journal of Nutrition; the flavanols inside can also protect you from the harmful effects of UV rays. The catch? The catch? (There is a catch, of course.) You have to eat chocolate with a cacao value of over 70 percent to reap any benefits. Move away from the Milky Way, in other words.

9. Edamame

Wherever possible, slate unprocessed soy into your diet for ethereal skin. Research published in the Journal of Nutritional Science and Vitaminology shows that only three months of daily use will protect you from wrinkles. To make sure you eat unprocessed soy, go for edamame: without steaming and salting, the delicious green bee is as competitive as soy, as you can find.

10. Olive oil

Like all, too much olive oil is no-go; only one tablespoon has approximately 120 calories that can add up quickly. Just a drizzle, and it's not okay — it's advisable. Studies show that olive oil antioxidants have been shown to stop aging defects and wrinkles. Moreover, olive oil is one of the 40 Heart Foods to Eat After 40 due to its high amount of BP-stabilizing "nitro fatty acids."

11. Grapefruit

You may well be aware of the cold boom of vitamin C. But, you may not be aware that vitamin C is a true superhero in the field of skin health: the nutrient also helps protect the skin cells from early death and helps to enhance collagen production. You might think of oranges as a great source when it comes to loading vitamin C – and it is! Grapefruit takes the cake; only one grapefruit has a recommended value of more than 100 percent per day for adults.

12. Mangos

Mangos, like grapefruits, are filled with vitamin C; in addition, only half a mango needs to be taken to reach the 100 percent mark. In addition, mangos contain carotenoids that shield you against the harmful effects of UV rays.

13. Kiwis

Kiwis are a vitamin C sleeper source, too: One cup of peeled Kiwi (if only because the skin is fluffy and odd, we suggest steering clear) contains more nutrients than one cup of oranges.

14. Papayas

A related orange fruit, Papayas, can also take a good dose of Vitamin C. But we suggest that you consume them at least; papaya has more sugar than other foods rich in vitamin C.

15. Lemons

Lemons alone definitely have no more vitamin C than oranges. (The orange size of a lemon has about 500 mg up to 30 mg of a lemon.) But lemons can form part of your culinary repertoire if you want healthy skin. One thing is that you can quickly add citrus to several dishes — from a complicated grilled fish to a plain glass of water. On the other hand, lemon juice is also a part of several en mode skincare products.

16. Oranges

Boring, yes, but this classic vitamin C fruit is an easy way to load up.

17. Lentils

Lentils are an excellent source of balanced, lean protein, such as sardines and Greek yogurt. But there are also lentils full of vitamin B9, which has been found to support your mane in two main ways: avoiding early graying and balding.

18. Grass-fed beef

An iron deficiency may be one of the culprits of thinning hair. The prime function of the nutrient is to transfer oxygen into the blood and cells of your body. And, when iron levels are small, hair follicles — the sort of cell that develops individual strands — don't get the oxygen they need to do their job. Battle this phenomenon with slating more iron-rich beef into your diet. Just make sure you get the grass-fed variety; you'll enjoy the Omega-3's heart-healthy benefits and skip the high fat inside processed beef.

19. Eggs

Vegetarians — and other people who can not or do not eat meat — think of eggs. Besides being rich in hair-enforcing iron, they are also a great source of biotin; a B-vitamin believed to help prevent age-related nails from becoming brittle and damaged.

20. Blueberries

Any type of berries contains antioxidants, but blueberries make your buck the best. According to the Molecular Nutrition & Food Science report, anthocyanins – which make blueberries blue – help to reduce the 'photography' of UV exposure. In other words, they can turn the clock back on small wrinkles and defects. (Not to mention the vitamin C skin-firming is a healthy source of blueberries.)

21. Strawberries

Strawberries are filled with polyphenols with highly influenced anti-aging effects, including increased development of collagen. (And yes, strawberries are a good source of vitamin C like blueberries.)

22. Blackberries

The special anthocyanins in blackberries will help to reduce the scar, according to a study conducted in Food and Function. If you have accumulated a series of battle wounds over the years, store the bumpy berries. (One cup is also a good source of Vitamin C every day.)

23. Cranberries

As you grow old, your teeth become weaker. Ingest a daily dose of cranberries to keep them healthier for longer. In Archives Oral Biology, cranberries can help prevent "dentine erosion"—or eventual tooth cracking and chipping in plain aging. According to the report. (Cranberries are not a decent source of vitamin C for what it's worth.)

24. Almonds

A decent quantity of protein can be contained in any nut, but almonds have the highest protein/calorie ratio. In addition, the almonds are filled with copper (helping to avoid graying), biotin (firming up aged clay), and vitamin E (helping to preserve the tint and beauty of the hair as you grow old).

25. Almond butter

Today, almond oil is a hair product that is increasingly popular. But eating it can also make your hair shine with high levels of Vitamin E. Just four tablespoons give you the required daily nutrient value. (To get that number, you will need 16 tablespoons of peanut butter.)

26. Sweet potatoes

Eat something equally white in the skin that glows like sunlight: sweet potatoes. According to a survey conducted in the Journal Evolution and Human Behaviour, the delicious tater can enhance the skin tint. And it's definitely not a pretext not to chow down; the ten healthy carbs that will not derail your six-pack are also sweet potatoes.

27. Cinnamon

More and more people are using cinnamon oil to plump hair these days. (If you find thinning hairs, inquire about items for your living room.) But eating cinnamon can also improve your hair. Mount Sinai Hospital researchers have pinpointed cinnamon as a follicle stimulator because, like iron, it may help your body transfer oxygen.

28. Carrots

No, carrots do not help your dream to change. (This crackpot hypothesis was ignored about as many times as it was posed.) However, carrots can help improve your skin. According to nutrient analysis, the use of carrots is related to the increased development of collagen. Don't eat too much, or you're going to turn brown. (Just kidding, that guy, too, is as dumb as the theory of sight-enhancing.)

29. Acai

The Acai Berry Extract can help promote skin cell regeneration, according to a report in Toxicology Research. This superfood is also high in belly fiber, making it the ideal way to start your day.

30. Kale

Kale is filled with vitamin K, which can help avoid and, in some cases, reverse skin decoloration according to studies from the Laser and Skin Surgery Center in New York.

31. Oysters

According to a study carried out by the Faculty of Medicine of the Imperial College, zinc is an important nutrient to repair damaged skin cells. One of the most frequent sources of zinc is oysters.

32. Steel-cut oatmeal

Yeah, oatmeal is a fantastic source of zinc (which improves skin health), but it's also a perfect way to take your daily dose of iron. Go to steel-cut oatmeal with less refined sugars than normal ones. Then add a healthy portion of antioxidant-packed berries to your bowl for optimum age-defying benefits.

33. Broccoli sprouts

There was strong support for the health benefits of broccoli, the least favorite food of any child (and some adults). But if you'd like to turn the clock back, eat more broccoli. Some researchers estimate that they have more than ten times the antioxidants of plain old broccoli.

34. Cheese

Think of cheese as tasty and nutritious toothpaste. According to a study in General Dentistry, the pH levels of their mouths return to brushed status after eating cheese people who refrained from brushing their teeth for two days. The major cause of decoloration associated with aging? Out-of-whack, high pH acidity. You do the math.

35. Whole wheat options

Any health-conscious person will tell you that swapping your beans for whole wheat options should be Step 1 in healthier lifestyles where possible. Yet, in addition to well-documented cardiovascular and abdominal advantages, whole grains will help you age in turn. Skyrocketing of processed carbohydrates — white bread and their ilk — allows the body to transform sugar into collagen-disturbing glucose. The effect is not caused by unrefined carbon — whole wheat bread, pasta, that sort of thing.

36. Pumpkin (and pumpkin seeds)

The American Journal of Clinical Nutrition says that when it comes to protecting you naturally from the adverse effects of ultraviolet exposure, few items do like beta-carotene, with which pumpkins are filled. And don't throw the remains out after you get your load. Because of its high levels of manganese, which are known to improve the production of collagen, pumpkin seeds are a true culinary holy grail.

37. Sockeye salmon

As mentioned, protein helps prevent your muscles from deteriorating prematurely. Most (edible) maritime creatures are full of nutrients, particularly sardines if you remember them. But let's face it: Sardines are totally disgusting. This protein, like salmon, can be obtained from a tastier source. Go for the variety of sockeye with more omega-3s and less saturated fat.

38. Tuna

Tuna is an excellent muscle builder, like most fish. But the fish have a hidden advantage overage. The unsaturated fatty acids in tuna will help reduce the prominence of wrinkles by conducting research of the Department of Food Science and Nutrition at Pukyong National University.

39. Roasted turkey

Among the protein-to-fat ratios, turkey is one of the best foods to consume. You can get just about 6 grams of fat per 24 grams of protein. Make sure you roast yours so that you won't end up in the platter with any needless butter filled with calories or oils.

40. Chicken

Turkey may be the best dog — or bird — for protein, but chicken is a near second. You should get a little less than 7 grams of fat per 24 g of protein (if you stay clear of the skin).

41. Watercress

You can find the usual suspects when it comes to antioxidant and vitamin-filled foods: kale, berries, and the other common fruits and veggies. But do not sleep on watercress: Vitamins A, B1, B2, B6, C, E, and K keep the skin plump. It has vitamins A, B1, and B2.

42. Pineapple

Like pumpkin seeds, pineapple is a perfect manganese source – so you really should load up the nutrient. Research in dermatology shows that a lack of manganese will cause the skin to prune faster.

43. Green tea

You'd like to drink more green tea because you don't want dentures. According to a report in the Journal Of Preventative Medicine, only a cup of sugar-free green tea (yes, that's the fish) prevented irreversible dental loss among elderly adults. We suggest you exchange one of your regular cups of coffee for a cup of green tea, both coffee drinks. (And no unnecessary coffee stains can be caused by green tea.)

44. Rooibos tea

Rooibos tea is also a fantastic anti-aging drink, but not as resistant to age as its green tea counterpart. Rooibos tea is full of polyphenols that protect the skin from early irritation and defects.

45. Beer

Yeah, to be extreme. Silicium thought to improve blood circulation to your scalp – and hair follicles – is more present in beer than almost any other beverage on the earth, according to a report in the Journal of Food Science and Agriculture. And if anyone doubts the habit of your beer, tell them it's science-supported. (Well, of course, within reason.) Cheers.

46. Cherry juice

Puffy hair, sallow skin, a reduced demeanor — skipping out on sleep is a sure way to age yourself instantly. So fight that every night by drinking a glass of fresh cherry juice. According to a report in the American Journal of Therapeutics, one nightly glass of the stuff will, on average, add almost an hour-and-a-half to a person's evening rest.

47. Tahini

Tahini is rich in polyunsaturated fats, and B vitamins that plump skin and strengthen hair. Don't know where to find it? For some freshly made hummus, hit up your nearest Mediterranean joint. It is a really essential ingredient. (Don't go for the store-bought products that seem to have extra unhealthy oils and sugars.)

48. Cucumbers

Water will help the skin remain radiant, according to the University of Wisconsin School of Medicine and Public Health. Regular ingestion of H2O prevents drying of the skin; long stretches of dry skin will reduce the natural glow of your skin. Eat cucumbers for a good source of water — which, as a bonus, will help dampen any skin-related inflammation per research in the Journal of Aging Science and Clinical Practice.

49. Watermelon

Need a good source of water? It's in the name.

50. Water

Naturally, the very best water source — yes, even more than cucumbers and watermelon — on the planet is, well, water! Consume at least six 8 ounce glasses a day for better bets.

THE BEST SKIN CARE PRODUCTS FOR YOUR 40S

You have reached an inflection point as you hit your 40's. It is the time of your life when you are really starting to see the effects of aging on your skin. Whether from years of exposure to the sun or from the lines of laughter that no longer disappear when you stop smiling, you realize your skin doesn't look like it used to. But that's no reason to worry, because in this diverse decade and beyond, you are still capable of having the best skin possible. With the right combination of powerful products and healthy ingredients, each of you can turn your skin to make it look better than it did ten years ago and keep it from getting older.

That's because Dr. Schultz has known the skin for decades, so now you too can. From over 180,000 patient visits, he's taken his expertise and poured it into products that make your skincare a no-brainer. So you're well on your way to your best skin ever with a little knowledge from Dr. Schultz and ingredients which deliver real results.

AVERAGE 40-YEAR-OLD WOMAN FACE

You will note variations in tone and texture in the face of a typical 40-year-old woman. You may think aging is all about wrinkles immediately, but that's usually only because they're the easiest changes to identify. In fact, when it comes to the skin, aging appearance, tone, and texture compensate for far more than wrinkles do. Dr. Schultz says, "When people come to my office to tell me, 'I need a pick-up,' what they're really saying is that they're frustrated with what they see in the mirror. And they say 'I need a Botox treatment' because I reply 'I can give you a Botox treatment, but it won't make you happy.' Because what I'm saying is that removing lines and wrinkles alone won't solve the issue you see in the mirror."

As we referred to above, by looking at these three categories, you can understand why your skin looks older: tones, texture, and contours. Everyone knows the contour problems such as curves, wrinkles, and creases, but surprisingly those represent just 5 percent of what you see in the mirror. The other 95 percent is the mixture of problems with tone and texture. Tone problems in the tint of your skin are discolorations like reds and browns. The reds may be either from damaged capillaries or from red blotches. The browns may be individual brown spots on your face, such as age spots, liver spots, or even brown blotches. And then we've got the all-important questions about texture. Texture problems rob your skin of luster and light, causing it to be dull, smooth, flaccid, and large-pored. They even end up depriving the skin of its smoothness.

Dr. Schultz uses this example of the relative value of tone and texture problems compared to lines: He says, "Think about a pilled, dirty, wrinkled shirt and then iron out the wrinkles. What's left in you? A dirty shirt lined up. And I think you'll have a far clearer picture of what you're doing the next time you look in the mirror, and you'll know it's not all about wrinkles.'

UNDERSTANDING ANTI-AGING

Dead cells continue to adhere to the surface of your skin as you age to form mounds. Such mounds are part of what makes your skin look older in terms of its color, texture, and contour. The presence of skin aging is primarily caused by the havoc created by dead cells on your skin. And the solution to this devastation? Exfoliation. Exfoliation. You may know something about physical exfoliation, but it is probably your best bet to pick a chemical exfoliant. Dr. Schultz says, "Physical exfoliation acts like sandpaper by scraping [dead skin cells] off the surface. Chemical exfoliation works safely and efficiently by dissolving the bond between cells, so they fall off faster. "Once cell mounds fall off, they expose your cleaner (and thus younger) skin.

BEST SKIN CARE ROUTINE FOR 40S

Three basic skincare items are the perfect regimen for your 40s: exfoliants, antioxidants, and sunscreen. As described above, exfoliants remove the glue that keeps on your face dead skin cells that produce uneven cloth. Antioxidants can help to lighten your skin and even your tone and protect you from free radicals that can lead to oxidative damage. You can reverse the signs of aging in both products to achieve a clear, smooth, firm skin. But you must still use sunscreen to avoid over-exposure to the sun if you want to protect yourself from further harm. These three items will form the basis for any serious routine of skincare.

7 THINGS DERMATOLOGISTS WANT YOU TO DO BEFORE YOU TURN 40

Any dermatologist will tell you that it's never too early to start taking care of your skin, but the sooner you develop a diet, the better. Miami-based dermatologist and cofounder, Dr. Loretta skincare Loretta Ciraldo, MD, FAAD, said, "Generally, prevention is more productive than correction." This is to include some morning and nighttime rituals in your 20s and 30s so that as you hit your 40s, you are more likely to have smoother, tighter, healthier skin.

According to Ciraldo, long before any deep lines or sunspots appear, it is important to use brightening and anti-wrinkle products, because the shift in microscopy like over pigment and loss of collagen begins in the 20s and progresses so gradually that you typically don't notice it until your 30s and 40s. At this point, they are much more difficult to handle.

Simultaneously, there is so much advice in the world on skincare that distilling the essential behaviors before 40 can be difficult. Not to mention the hard-core anti-aging services that you can find in a dermatologist's office or skin health spa can be time-consuming, costly, and (if you are mainly skinny) not enjoyable. In your twenties and thirties, dermatologists accept that you will conform to what you actually find doable and pleasant — or you will not adhere to it, and it will not work. 'Adopt skincare practices which you love,' says Craig Kraffert, the dermatologist-certified board and Chairman of Amarte Skin Care. "If your skincare routine isn't fun, consistency is difficult. Pick high-quality items and carefully choose your active ingredients."

What are the main skincare items, ingredients, and behaviors to be implemented before 40?

1. GET ACQUAINTED WITH VITAMIN C

Dermatologists believe that antioxidant vitamin C is one of the essential components to use in your 20s and 30s, as this helps avoid dark spots before they occur. "Vitamin C is a great lightener with many advantages, as it improves collagen and also benefits from antioxidants and UV defense," says Ciraldo.

Audrey Kunin, a dermatologist with the DermaDoctor certification in boards of experts, suggests searching for high-power vitamin C serum with ferulic acid vitamin E antioxidant boosters, such as DermaDoctor Kakadu C ($95) or SkinCeuticals tried-and-true C E Ferulic ($166). Apply your vitamin C for extra protection in the morning before moisturizer and sunscreen.

If your skincare routine doesn't please, it's difficult to start.

2. EXFOLIATE TWO OR THREE TIMES A WEEK

As if the existential tension of growing older was not enough: "The maturing skin gets thicker, gray, drab, lifeless, and the pores get bigger," says Kunin. Why is this happening? As Ciraldo states, not as easy as we are, our dead skin cells shed. This makes the skin look white and the texture rough. In addition, the excess pigment is retained in dead cells so that your skin tone can appear discolored or irregular.

Fortunately, two or three exfoliating times a week will help to overcome or at least stave off some of these issues. "Chemical and physical exfoliation will help shut the issue down before it starts and help preserve your youthful luminosity," says Kunin. Bonus: Daily exfoliation also allows your other skincare items to penetrate even better, including your vitamin C serum.

For physical exfoliators, we fan Amarte 's gentle, maize seed Regular Exfoli Powder ($37), great for sensitive skin; we swear AHA and BHA masks, peels, and serums, particularly Renée Rouleau's Pore + Wrinkle ($50) for chemical exfoliations and exfoliation.

3. MAKE SUNSCREEN THE CENTERPIECE OF YOUR ROUTINE

If you add one anti-aging skin care product to your daily routine, require it to be sunscreen. "It is never too late to start wearing SPF every day," promises Kunin. "Even if you are a sun-seeker for your life, it's never too late to avoid more harm to the sky."

Consistency is the secret to the sunscreen — You just need to use at least SPF 30 per day (and preferably all day long) to keep your skin glowy, young and most importantly, healthy. "Apply every day with attention to accuracy on all exposed skin surfaces," says Kraffert. "Additional to the face, these include hands, bare forearms, neck (front, sides, back) and neckline."

We know that most people, including us, are shut down every day by using the sunscreen, because most formulations are dense, chalky, and crack you out. But, Supergoop, we swear! Two Byrdie editor-approved items that will inspire you are Unseen Sunscreen ($32) and EltaMD UV Transparent Facial Sunscreen ($35).

4. EMBRACE MOISTURIZING EMOLLIENTS

As we age, the skin is drier, flakier, more brittle, and so you should be able to protect the moisture barrier early on. There are a handful of highly successful dermatologists who prescribe moisturizing ingredients like moisture-trapping lipids, which imitate natural skin lipids that make the skin smooth and silky, but which can deteriorate over time. Ciraldo manufactures an Extreme Refilling Serum ($70), which has "biological skin lipids and a super-strong antioxidant known as Lipochrome." However, Ciraldo is also recommending the lipid-containing CeraVe drugstore cream at a super-accessible price.

The other moisturizing ingredient all dermis suggest is sodium hyaluronate, a hyaluronic acid derivative because it recreates the lubrication of the hyaluronic acid which our skin produces naturally. It is excellent for dry, aging skin and wrinkle reduction, and particularly for the aging eye area.

5. START GETTING HEAD-TO-TOE SKIN CHECKS

Looking younger is cool and cool, but it's better to ensure that your skin is safe from cancer. Therefore, it is wise to get a full-body inspection by a dermatologist once a year, or more if melanoma takes place in your family. "Now is the time to have your dermatologist test the skin in the baseline to ensure that there are no early signs of pre-cancerous skin changes," says Kunin. "In its early stages, it is still much better to capture something than to bear the consequences later on."

6. INCORPORATE RETINOL INTO YOUR ROUTINE

Just like in your daily routine, vitamin C should have a place; retinol should have a place at night. Derms agree that your 20s are the best time to start using retinol of high quality at night, as the Vitamin A derivative acts to avoid wrinkles and promote collagen development.

Retinol is a bit of a finicky ingredient, so be sure to select a product that comes in an opaque, well-secured bottle that does not expose it to sunlight because it is not safe to picture or sunlight. As retinol can also irritate the skin, use it for one or two days a week and then work your way before you use it at night.

7. Care for the skin morning and night of your head, and remember, if anything else, wash your beautiful face.

Just as you brush your teeth, it isn't enough just once a day to care for your skin. Since daytime skincare is about protecting your face and skincare at night is about fixing it, it is important to set up a routine before going to bed and to wake up (including the ingredients and the advice above, of course).

And whatever you do, make sure your skin is cleansed, morning and night. Plastic surgeon Z, according to Manhattan. Paul Lorenc, MD, if you have the ability to do only one thing in front of your house, you can "remove excess dirt from daylight." Unwashed skin means blocked pores, dull, broken teeth, overall, faster aging. So start here and reverse your direction.

HOW YOUR MINDSET CAN CHANGE HOW YOU AGE

We face aging with good-looking slogans, which carry platitudes into a knife battle. "I'm young for 70 years! "We say, overlooking the fact that the average life expectancy in the United States is not going to be much until we're 78 years old. "Fifty is the new 40," we say to ourselves, "It is not because there is no statistical truth. The latest 49 1/2 will never be fifty.

Then comes a little insight, which appears, if anything, to be the most educated of all: "You're just as old as you feel." As you feel, it's the twin defects of being both insignificant and blameful – as if feeling old is your own fault. However, it turns out that someone who coined that one may have been on something large.

It's no longer hidden that your familiar mind-body breaks into the abstract, the ethereal, and your flesh into the chaotic and mechanical. Everybody affects your moods, emotions, and ideas. Learn to relax, and your blood pressure goes down; recover from depression, and the immune system wakes up; take a pharmacologically inexpensive sugar pill that is supposed to be a strong headache, backache, or infection treatment, and as if you were suddenly getting better.

The boring question was always this: If the mind can cure the body, can it also rejuvenate it? Can it make the aging process physically, measurably younger, or at least slow? People who are already researching these things agree that the way we think and feel will boost the population of stick-fighting white blood cells and lower blood pressure levels of the hormone, why does it not help to regenerate bones or reverse heart disease or maintain age-decompressed brain cells? "You're just as old as you sound," might just be part of the equation. With justification, you might be as old as you are, as research builds up your attitude, your temperament, and, honestly, how optimistic you are not just about how you feel but also how your cells mature.

"Let's view mind and body as words," says Ellen Langer, a psychology professor at Harvard University and since the late 1970s studied aging, treatment, decision-making, and wellbeing. "Let them be put together like one thing and say wherever you put the mind; you put the body as well."

When you make a move, the medical tool kit gets far bigger. Not only do it include pharmacology and service, but also things like meditation, creativity, resilience, and social interaction – all these things are often far from the observable wavelength of medicine but unexpectedly find a place comfortably in it.

Consider, for example, a study that shows that one day of consciousness meditation can downregulate a gene that codes for inflammation – one of the biggest aging engines. This also shows that the cellular damage from the extremely reactive oxygen atoms called free radicals can be minimized by reducing stress. Or the investigation which most remarkably found that the telomeres in your cells, the little cuffs which cap chromosomes and erode over your life span, will actually develop further if your mind is in the right condition.

"It's all about everyday behavior and choices we make," says Elissa Epel, a psychiatry professor at the University of California in San Francisco (UCSF), researching stress and aging. "We have an increasing number of world study showing that aging is not only an aspect of age but how we live." Deciding to live longer seems to be the same as choosing to live younger.

WINDING BACK THE MIND

It wasn't until the late 1970s that researchers began seriously talking about using the mind to stop the aging process, and it was Langer's seminal work in the counterclockwise direction that really started things. In 1979, just as she started to teach at Harvard, in her 1970s, she hired a party of eight people for a five-day retreat in New Hampshire. Men were neither good nor poor in health, but what was called age-appropriate health, that is, sluggish, flexible, and easily tired. Still, Langer was eager to make a difference.

The retreat, as the men learned when they arrived, was an old monastery that looked like the world did in 1959. Vintage programs on vintage TVs were shown. Music from the midcentury played on radios from the midcentury. The men were also handled as they should then have been – nobody tried to support them with their bags or to take a blanket for them. They conversed on subjects they addressed in 1959 – the events at the Eisenhower White House, say, or in front of the Dodgers – White Sox Series. And before men get an insight into themselves and break the spell, all the mirrors have been removed from space.

At the beginning and the end of the five-day cycle, Langers performed a series of physical and cognitive assessments for men, resulting as she predicted: their performance improved significantly on virtually every single measure, and was in many cases similar to what men predicted a decade or two to be.

"The study spoke about the potential for improving our wellbeing," says Langer. "We just can't promise we will look at any point. You want things to get easier when you're 20, and you hurt your hand. You have bought into the mental state that you fall apart when you're 70, and then you do it.

Langer checked the same idea in a different manner. After a large group of hotel maids who struggled against their weight, she said half of the study that studies found that the work she did every day was a vigorous way to burn calories. No such knowledge was given to the other women. The women who felt their exercises were a workout lost more weight than those in the other category at the end of the test.

As persuasive as they are, Langer's studies are not complete. They work very well to show that young people want to make their bodies young – or at least younger – but don't know why. Langer herself is metaphysical rather than analytical. "The process is the aspect that people find so difficult to understand," she says. "But no mediator is required if the mind and body are one."

Maybe. Maybe. But, even though other scientists don't need a mediator, they are working hard, beginning in human cells, on telomeres.

THE LEVERS OF AGING

Telomeres burn down like a kind of candlewick over the course of a lifetime, leaving the chromosomes susceptible to damage and beginning the aging cycle.

Researchers had known the fundamentals of telomeres since 1978, when postdoctoral fellow Elizabeth Blackburn, now at UCSF, first mapped their structure and later their work with her Harvard collaborator Jack Szostak. In 1984, Blackburn and her graduate student Carol Greider discovered the enzyme telomerase, now at the Johns Hopkins School of Medicine, which fixes and preserves telomeres — at least when it's around at adequate amounts. When those rates fall, which happens when we get older, we kick off the aging cycle. The discovery won the 2009 Nobel Prize for Medicine for every three of them.

"If the studies look at which individuals will die in the next three years," Blackburn says, "if the telomeres are shorter, the odds are greater. Shorting telomeres play into cardiovascular disease, problems with the immune system, and possibly diabetes by affecting beta cells in the pancreas – though it has been seen only in mouse models so far.

The question is, are there ways of intervening to protect the telomeres and your health? The response – at least preliminary – is yes, and the reduction of stress is one important process. In 2014, Epel and her colleague Eli Puterman, also from UCSF, over the course of a year, examined 239 fits, postmenopausal women. Many of the subjects encountered at least one of 13 major life stressors, including family homelessness, financial problems, divorce, and a child's disease.

At the beginning and end of the year, the length of their telomeres was measured, and the more life stressors these women encountered during that period, the shorter their telomeres were that year. But some of the women still had positive health behaviors – they were exercising, eating well, and sleeping well. The women who also followed positive health practices consistently extended the length of their telomeres. "The issue has always been whether the telomeres adapt to changes in the everyday lifestyle, or whether the system is constant and continues at its own rate," says Epel. "It was a lifestyle in our research, with the harm occurring mainly in sedentary people."

Worse, older people are not limited to telomere-shortening tension, and they don't even have to witness it firsthand. Epel cites research showing that the babies whose mothers had undergone more pain when they were pregnant displayed shorter telomeres when cord blood is drawn from newborns than those whose moms had an easier pregnancy. "We've repeated the original finding," she says, "and it indicates the healthy telomere maintenance does not begin when you are born, but before you are born."

Some researchers believe changes in exercise and other healthy behaviors will increase telomerase production, and animal experiments in test tubes show that increased telomerase that, in effect, result in the growth of telomeres. However, telomerase supplements – whether manufactured synthetically or in the many herbal supplements claiming to contain the enzyme – are not the solution. If telomeres never burn down, you get immortal cells, which is another way that cancer cells can be told.

"Cancers love telomerase, and some cancers are up-regulating it like mad," Blackburn says. "But certain cancers often contribute to low telomerase as that makes telomeres less stable." Attempting to improve telomerase by supplements is a very risky game to play — at least considering the current state of medical knowledge. "We do not know how to strike that form of balance. My impression would be that I am playing with fire if I take something that would drive my telomerase up, "Blackburn says.

PUTTING OUT FIRES

Telomeres aren't the only major players in the aging game who have to do with tension. Chronic inflammation is another. The sympathetic nervous system, which is not known for thinking things too well, thinks you're about to meet a predator or some other life-threatening obstacle when you're anxious. And the brain sends a signal to the adrenal gland to begin to secrete the hormones epinephrine and cortisol; these hormones together signal the immune system to release proteins known as inflammatory cytokines. These prepare the white blood cells and other warriors for infection to rush to an imminent wound site.

That works very well when there's a wound, or when the danger is brief, and you're running away without injury. Either way, the machine is dialing itself back down due mainly to cortisol. But what if you're not primed for some kind of battle — with your boss, your family, your credit card statements — and the body is still inundated with inflammatory chemicals? The body suffers from what is known as inflammation in such cases – and this is terrible.

"There is no invader as with a wound, but we respond as if there were any way," Epel says. "That creates a pleasant environment for cancer, weakening of the brain, cardiovascular disease," in other words, for many of the key aging killers.

One of the best ways to combat this is by meditation and mindfulness exercises, with a balanced mental state. Researchers are increasingly finding that a specific type of meditation known as Mindfulness-Based Stress Reduction (MBSR)–which, as its name implies, involves paying careful attention to emotions, thoughts and other sensations while meditating – can relax an inflamed immune system in the same way that it can relax an inflamed mood.

In 2013, a neuroscientist and director of the Healthy Minds Research Center at the University of Wisconsin in Madison, Richard Davidson, conducted a couple of studies showing how strong an impact MBSR can have on the body. In one, he and his collaborators compared 40 subjects–21 of which participated in eight hours of a mixture of guided meditation, meditative walks, and meditation lectures, and 19 participated in similarly calming yet non-meditation practices. At the end of a period as short as eight hours, the meditators displayed a decline in the expression of the very genes that control inflammation, which also suggests a decline in inflammation itself.

Over the course of eight weeks, another test repeated the results, and in the end, the experimenters used a suction tool to lift a tiny blister on the participants' heads. When the fluid was removed, the meditators displayed substantially lower levels of inflammatory cytokines – the same cytokines that do so much harm when they are continuously circulating in the body.

"The daily use of certain contemplative approaches tends to be able to shift the course of age-related shifts," says Davidson. "Some studies also show that meditation can delay the decline of gray matter in the brain related to age."

Davidson understates stuff on this latter level. Exciting research reported from UCLA in February compared two study groups of 50 men, ranging from 24 to 77 years of age – a strong demographic slice because gray matter generally starts to decline when we're in our 20s. One community consisted of people who did not meditate, the other people who had been daily meditators for four to 46 years in every position. The brains of all 100 participants were tested with magnetic resonance imaging, and the findings were unmistakable: in many regions of the brain, the meditators displayed less gray matter loss relative to the non-meditators.

"We were anticipating very small and distinct effects found in some of the regions traditionally associated with meditation," said Dr. Florian Kurth, the study's co-author. "Rather, what we really found was a widespread meditation phenomenon that encompassed regions all over the brain."

THE OPTIMISM EFFECT

Simple optimism is almost as strong as meditation – and definitely simpler for people who would be perfectly content to set aside time for solitary reflection in a quiet place if they can find the hour and the location and the peace. Challenges and failures, and even disasters, are non-negotiable aspects of life, but how you face them is what's negotiable.

Dr. Hilary Tindle, a physicist and clinical researcher at Vanderbilt University, has developed a body of work on the connection between attitude and wellbeing, both of which point to the unexpected power of being only positive. Tindle collected data from 97,253 women who had completed questionnaires for the Women's Health Initiative of the National Institutes of Health in one major 2009 survey, seeking to link hopefulness and mortality. Women who scored high on optimism – hoping for the future – showed results had substantially lower levels of heart disease, cancer, and mortality compared to women who scored high on pessimism.

Tindle also researched cynicism, which can be defined as other people's feelings of pessimism, believing them to be untrustworthy and even harmful. Women with lower cynicism had a lower risk of death compared to those who treated most of the others with skepticism.

She compared over 430 people who had undergone coronary bypass surgery in a 2012 study–284 of whom were diagnosed with at least low-level clinical depression and 146 of whom did not. The participants all took the same survey of optimism the research group had in the other report. The discouraged pessimists had more than double the risk of complication and rehospitalization as opposed to the positive community within eight months of surgery.

"My goal as a doctor is to help people appreciate the relationship better than they do," says Tindle. "But they need to do so in such a way as to make it workable. In other words, how do we implement all these new findings? That is the critical question, in the end.

Researchers are divided on how it is possible for people who have made it pessimistic or depressed or sedentary in the middle ages to undo all the damage to their environments by a change in attitude and meditation alone. But work is piling up that it can help – and it can't hurt for sure. For most health issues, the most important thing is a lifestyle – food, exercise, adequate sleep, and positive thinking.

That's not glamorous, but take what works and what makes headlines when it comes to longevity. The truth is the older odometer never runs backward. The 70-year-old is about ten years older than the 60-year-old. But if you think about how many years these two men have left, put your money on a positive, healthy 70 over a cynical, sedentary '60s. That, if nothing else, puts a nice twist on the harsh law that all lives must end: enjoy the time you have, and you may just get more.

CONCLUSION

Pollution, lifestyle, and nutrition are the main factors in how we remain healthy and aging. Pollution's main effect on our bodies is the increased development of free radicals in our cells, which weakens the immune system. As a result, we have a higher chance of premature aging and chronic conditions such as asthma and cancer emerging. Antioxidants mop up free radicals and can be contained or used as a dietary supplement in some fruits and vegetables. Smoking is also a significant factor in premature aging. Look at your smoking friends and family and consider how they look at the same age non-smokers. Smokers usually have more facial lines and wrinkles and may discolor their teeth.

Drinking plenty of water is helping to flush toxins out of our body, particularly between meals. It also helps to keep the skin clear of imperfections and can prevent dehydration of the hangover headaches, and of course, water is calorie-free!

Take regular exercise to maintain a healthy heart and lungs, and improve your metabolic rate. Every day, a brisk 30-minute walk will burn off calories and help develop healthy bones. Break the day in your lunchtime with a half-hour walk, and you might lose the equivalent of one stone of weight each year. Do you have to drive to work or to the store, really? The support that the pollution caused by automobile emissions, if possible, by walking or cycling. Get out and discover your surrounding environment. Lovely walks can be made in local parks or along canal paths. Ask the neighbors, or search on an Ordnance Survey map for footpaths and bridleways.

A diet rich in antioxidants can help reduce pollution's impact on our health. Some health experts think the cause of premature aging is free radical damage. Most of us know that by using a UV blocker, we can shield our skin from the sun to reduce the aging effects of the sun. But how many of us are aware of the aging impact toxins can have on our complexions? Naturally rich in antioxidants, nutritious foods include beetroot, blueberries, brussels sprouts, broccoli, cod, carrots, cherries, cranberries, grapes, prunes, peppers, raspberries, spinach, strawberries, sweet potatoes, and tomatoes. Co-enzyme Q10, lipocortin, lycopene, pycnogenol, and selenium are nutritional supplements that contain antioxidants to help protect against harmful free radicals. It could be bought from health food stores.

Do Not Go Yet; One Last Thing To Do

If you enjoyed this book or found it useful, I'd be very grateful if you'd post a short review on Amazon. Your support does make a difference, and I read all the reviews personally so I can get your feedback and make this book even better.

Thanks for your help and support!